Military Trucks

Julie Murray

Abdo Kids Junior
is an Imprint of Abdo Kids
abdobooks.com

Abdo
TRUCKS AT WORK
Kids

abdobooks.com

Published by Abdo Kids, a division of ABDO, P.O. Box 398166, Minneapolis, Minnesota 55439. Copyright © 2024 by Abdo Consulting Group, Inc. International copyrights reserved in all countries. No part of this book may be reproduced in any form without written permission from the publisher. Abdo Kids Junior™ is a trademark and logo of Abdo Kids.

Printed in the United States of America, North Mankato, Minnesota.

052023

092023

THIS BOOK CONTAINS RECYCLED MATERIALS

Photo Credits: Getty Images, Shutterstock, US Army, US Navy, ©mark6mauno p.7/ CC BY 2.0, ©U.S. Pacific Fleet p.11/ CC BY-NC 2.0, ©The JIDA p.22/ CC BY-NC 2.0, ©U.S. Pacific Fleet p.22/ CC BY-NC 2.0, ©U.S. Indo-Pacific Command p.22/ CC BY-NC-ND 2.0, ©New York National Guard p.22/ CC BY-ND 2.0

Production Contributors: Teddy Borth, Jennie Forsberg, Grace Hansen

Design Contributors: Candice Keimig, Pakou Moua

Library of Congress Control Number: 2022946717

Publisher's Cataloging-in-Publication Data

Names: Murray, Julie, author.

Title: Military trucks / by Julie Murray

Description: Minneapolis, Minnesota : Abdo Kids, 2024 | Series: Trucks at work | Includes online resources and index.

Identifiers: ISBN 9781098266165 (lib. bdg.) | ISBN 9781098266868 (ebook) | ISBN 9781098267216 (Read-to-me ebook)

Subjects: LCSH: Trucks--Juvenile literature. | Vehicles--Juvenile literature. | Military transportation—Juvenile literature.

Classification: DDC 388.32--dc23

Table of Contents

Military Trucks 4

More
Military Trucks 22

Glossary 23

Index 24

Abdo Kids Code 24

Military Trucks

There are many military trucks. They are used for different things.

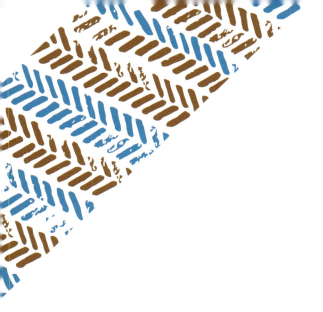

Some carry **supplies**.

Heavy Expanded Mobility Tactical Truck (HEMTT)

7

Some can travel over **rough** ground.

Some can move from ground to water!

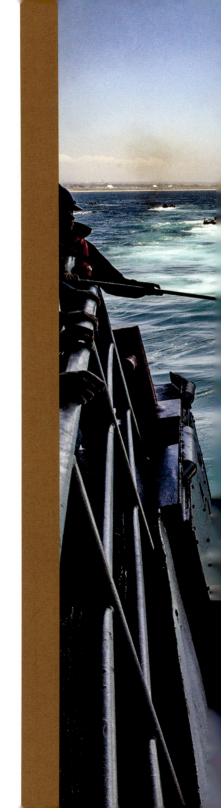

Amphibious Combat Vehicle

11

Some move soldiers from one place to another.

Heavy Mobility Multipurpose Wheeled Vehicle (HMMWV)

13

Some have heavy **armor**.

This protects soldiers.

Cougar 6x6 MRAP

15

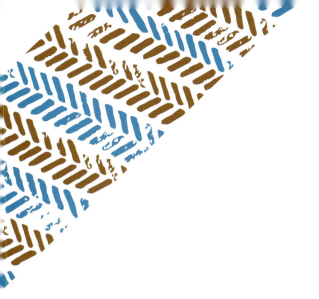

Fighting trucks are for **combat**.

Light Armored Vehicle (LAV)

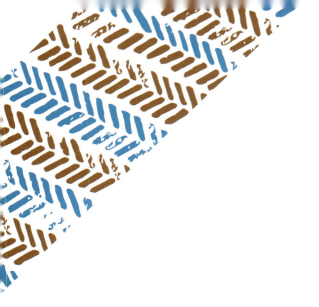

Some trucks have no driver.

They are remote controlled.

Autonomous Multi-Domain Launcher

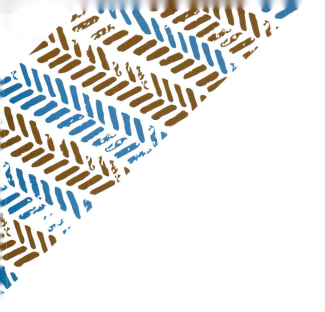
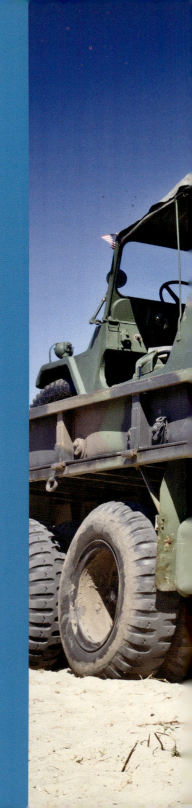

Have you seen any of these trucks?

M923A1 Cargo Truck

More Military Trucks

Buffalo Mine Protected Route Clearance Vehicle

Medium Tactical Vehicle Replacement (MTVR)

Stryker

Wrecker

Glossary

armor
a covering placed on vehicles that protects against weapons.

combat
fighting.

rough
having an uneven surface.

supplies
equipment or other essential things.

Index

armor 14

combat 16

remote control 18

soldiers 12, 14

supplies 6

transport 6, 12

uses 4, 6, 8, 10, 12, 14, 16

water 10

Visit **abdokids.com** to access crafts, games, videos, and more!

Use Abdo Kids code **TMK6165** or scan this QR code!